THE ENNEAGRAM

The Quest for Self Transcendence

by

Éilís Bergin PBVM
and
Eddie Fitzgerald SDB

Cover Art: H. Grabowski

Published and designed by:
SDB MEDIA, St. Teresa's Rd., Dublin 12
Phone: (01) 555605   Fax: (01) 558781

THE ENNEAGRAM

The Enneagram of personality types is almost as old as Christianity, originating in all probability in Afghanistan nearly 2,000 years ago. There has been a great deal of secrecy surrounding it and until this century it was handed down solely by word of mouth from Sufi master to individual disciple.

It is a sophisticated and practical method of helping people discover their inner selves, enabling them to deal with their problems, understand their family and friends and cope with the wide variety of interpersonal relationships which we all experience in the modern world.

These notes are designed to accompany an oral explanation of the Enneagram. They are not, therefore, on their own, an adequate introduction to such a complex and rich method of self-discovery as the Enneagram. Those who take our course will, we hope, find them helpful for reference.

Most of us find it difficult to face up to the negative elements in our personality. We prefer to emphasize the positive. Over the years we have built up defence mechanisms which enable us to block out our shadow side. Sometimes these are so ingrained that we are no longer consciously aware of them and consequently do not see them as a problem.

But, if we are ever going to discover our personality type and our true selves, it is vital that, like Luke Skywalker in the *Star Wars* film trilogy, we courageously face up to the dark side of ourselves, and seek healing and personal growth.

Éilís Bergin
Eddie Fitzgerald

ONES

1. I like everything to be as perfect as possible.
2. I work very hard to get rid of my faults.
3. I find I apologise a lot for all sorts of things.
4. The adjective which describes me best is probably 'finicky'.
5. It upsets me enormously when people aren't fair.
6. I always think I'm not good enough to merit other people's love.
7. I find it difficult to relax and take time out.
8. I have an inbuilt conscience which continually nags at me.
9. I identify with reformers and all those who fight for what's right.
10. Finding the least flaw in something puts me off.
11. I see things in terms of black or white rather than as shades of grey.
12. I rarely have enough time in which to do everything I need to do.
13. I get upset when things aren't the way they should be.
14. I'm a worrier.
15. I like to be right; I don't like to be wrong.
16. I resent it when people don't measure up to what they should be.
17. I can be very strict and puritanical at times.
18. I pay too much attention to details and minutiae.
19. I'm always finding fault and noticing what's missing.
20. When things go wrong I keep analysing precisely why.
21. I feel everyone should be honest, myself most of all.
22. I object strongly to wasting time.
23. I'm continually blaming myself for not being better.
24. I'm generally restless, striving continuously for what's beyond my grasp.
25. I am very resentful, sometimes unbearably so.

TWOS

1. I feel I'm always the one who's reaching out and giving.
2. Helping comes naturally to me.
3. People can get close to me.
4. I often feel empty inside.
5. I have the feeling that I'm not appreciated most of the time.
6. I'm the counsellor, advice-giver and sympathiser all rolled into one.
7. Being needed is important to me.
8. I can always be counted on to come to the rescue in a crisis.
9. Even my free time is given over to others.
10. Caring is my one big preoccupation.
11. I like to think I'm self sufficient.
12. I'm a flatterer.
13. I'd much rather give than receive.
14. It's possible that others think I'm very emotional.
15. Sometimes other people just 'use' me, and it gets to me.
16. I prefer not to dwell on my own needs and wants.
17. If I'm honest, I know I have a 'martyr complex'.
18. I feel good about myself when I help meet others' needs.
19. I'm proud of my service to others.
20. I resent my time being taken from me.
21. I don't get openly angry, but I do tend to manipulate.
22. I can become quite aggressive when people go against me.
23. My own needs are secondary to those of others.
24. People aren't always grateful for the trouble I take on their behalf.
25. I like to compliment people.

THREES

1. I move in the fast lane.
2. I'm a natural when it comes to plans and organisation.
3. I like to know where I fit in and what's expected of me.
4. I am an excellent team worker.
5. My image is important to me; I like others to see me as a success.
6. I can lose my identity when over-involved with work.
7. I live and breathe 'success'.
8. Plans can be more important than people.
9. I don't mind boasting about what I've done or who I've seen etc.
10. I'm a quick and efficient worker and am often envied in this regard.
11. I like to keep tabs on the progress I've made.
12. Failure is to be avoided at all costs.
13. I find I neglect my inner world.
14. I often have to compromise in order to get others to come with me.
15. I have no difficulty in decision making.
16. I think you need to be successful for others to take notice of you.
17. I am perfectly capable of bending the truth to suit my purposes.
18. I can be quite aggressive, especially with people who fail.
19. I tend to feel inferior if I'm not on top.
20. I like starting projects and then passing them on to others to finish.
21. I project a good image; I'd be great in advertising.
22. I know what I want and I set out to get it.
23. People mightn't believe it, but I do suffer from a fair bit of anxiety.
24. I'm very impressed by those who have achieved a lot in their lives.
25. I emphasize the positive and try not to remember my failures.

FOURS

1. I genuinely feel quite special.
2. Experiences go deeper with me than with most.
3. I tend to do things with panache and style.
4. I sometimes feel I'm locked in my past.
5. The symbolic in life attracts me.
6. I am often taken up with thoughts of loss, pain and death.
7. I find an emotional outlet in dramatic presentation or expression.
8. My mood swings from very high to very low; in between is dull.
9. People feel I look down on them and am somehow snobbish.
10. I'm no stranger to depression.
11. I often seem to whinge about what's going wrong in my life.
12. I frequently wish I had others' gifts and talents.
13. Anything that offends good taste offends me.
14. I am often misunderstood.
15. I like to surround myself with beautiful things.
16. I empathize so deeply with others that I can really feel their hurt.
17. Life is tough, but I try to smile away the tears.
18. I rarely think of myself as being ordinary.
19. I tend to avoid fuss in my dress.
20. I don't seem to be as happy as others are.
21. Many people are just not able to understand how I feel.
22. I'm more upset than most about the ending of relationships.
23. People think of me as being over-dramatic.
24. I often wonder if I react to situations with enough depth of feeling.
25. I appreciate most art forms and consider myself artistic.

FIVES

1. I'm often an observer rather than a participant.
2. I don't like sharing my feelings.
3. I need a lot of time to myself.
4. Giving comes hard to me. I prefer to accept, take and receive.
5. I tend to hoard what I know, because knowledge is precious.
6. I'm stingy with my time, and frugal with money.
7. I'm good at getting a detached overview of complex problems.
8. My motto for problem-solving is to 'think things through'.
9. I work best on my own.
10. Deep down, I'm scared of being empty.
11. I don't like to shout. It annoys me when I'm told to speak up.
12. I find it difficult to ask people to help me.
13. I dislike being short-changed in anything. I like value for money.
14. I'm not the pushy type.
15. I question everything to find out how things operate.
16. I rarely 'sugar the pill'; I sometimes lack tact.
17. I give the appearance of being cool, detached and above it all.
18. I mutter words like 'dope', 'nitwit', 'stupid', 'fool' when upset.
19. I'm happy to let others start the ball rolling.
20. I'm a magpie, picking up things which just might come in useful.
21. I find small talk difficult and can clam up in company.
22. The grand design is more important to me than the concrete details.
23. I tend to think issues through before discussing them.
24. I don't speak as much as others, so my views have to be asked for.
25. I'm non-plussed when asked to express my feelings.

SIXES

1. I'm generally balanced in my views.
2. I make very few spontaneous decisions.
3. Loyalty to the group is very important to me.
4. I am sensitive, 'touchy', and I don't like being crossed.
5. I often sacrifice my independence for security.
6. Fear looms large in my life.
7. I like knowing what is expected of me.
8. I take sides in an argument and always want to know who is on my side.
9. Without rules there's no knowing what people would get up to.
10. I'm often riddled with doubt.
11. I feel I'm a coward at times.
12. I'm quicker than most at spotting trouble and danger
13. My sense of duty often determines what I do or don't do.
14. I like to explore all the possibilities before taking action.
15. I support authority rather than go against it.
16. I come across to others as being a bit dogmatic.
17. I'm shy.
18. I often change my mind.
19. I'm often unaware of how direct I am, though I see it in others.
20. I am overly serious.
21. Indecision prevents me from achieving much good.
22. I feel inhibited in many ways.
23. I envy those who can make quick decisions.
24. I prefer to stick to a timetable than to leave things just happen.
25. I find I'm probably more defensive than most people.

SEVENS

1. Most people are too serious; if you lighten up you brighten up.
2. I want people to think of me as a fun person to be with.
3. I've rarely met a person I couldn't like.
4. I love to daydream.
5. I'm a good conversationalist, with a fund of stories to tell.
6. I try to avoid painful situations; if I'm hurt, I withdraw.
7. You can never have too much of a good thing.
8. I'm often complimented on being the life and soul of the party.
9. I'm very open to people - not suspicious or judgemental.
10. I was very happy as a child.
11. I like to get a quick response to requests - I hate waiting around.
12. I make great plans.
13. I'm much too optimistic a person to dwell on life's difficulties.
14. I'm very much a child at heart - playful and fun-loving.
15. I prefer my conversation light and cheerful, not serious and heavy.
16. I enjoy life to the full.
17. In spite of the hassle, things generally work out in the end.
18. Everything has its place in the grand design of the universe.
19. It's morbid to be sad for too long.
20. My plans are often a bit up in the air and short on concrete details.
21. I don't have the perseverance to match my enthusiasms.
22. People see me as superficial rather than substantial.
23. In my view the future holds great things in store for us.
24. I like things to be nice and pleasant.
25. I don't like confrontations; I prefer to paper over the cracks.

EIGHTS

1. I believe if you want something you should fight for it.
2. People don't scare me; if they need to be tackled, no problem.
3. I find it hard when I'm told I have to change.
4. People bring their problems on themselves.
5. I'm hard on people who hurt me and often punish them for it.
6. My initial response to requests is 'no'; it gives me time to analyse.
7. I'm a bit of a rebel; I don't always conform.
8. I'm a hard worker.
9. I enjoy power and using it.
10. I'm a bit coarse and crude at times - 'earthy' in the best sense.
11. If I am not satisfied I say so and make no bones about it.
12. In a group I always know who has the power and who has not.
13. I make decisions quickly, sometimes without having the full facts.
14. If things don't move along I soon get bored.
15. I'm not slow to exploit other's vulnerable points if necessary.
16. I can't 'let sleeping dogs lie'.
17. I'm very protective of those in my care.
18. I'm very strong on justice; injustice is unacceptable to me.
19. Introspection is frequently just a cop-out from action.
20. I'm a forceful person - a good adjective would be 'aggressive'.
21. I can make things happen and get projects finished.
22. I have a sensitive and tender side which I find hard to express.
23. I find it difficult to listen.
24. I am rough and abrasive, and can grind others down.
25. I find it difficult to trust myself.

NINES

1. People see me as relaxed; a good adjective would be 'easy-going'.
2. It's pointless getting too upset about things.
3. I try to pour oil on troubled waters by minimizing the problems.
4. I need a push to get started.
5. I have a great inner peace.
6. One of my great gifts is that I'm balanced and stable.
7. 'Mañana' (tomorrow) is a lovely word; things can always wait.
8. I generally take the easy way out.
9. I usually sleep very well.
10. "Let nothing disturb you" is a good motto.
11. Change upsets me a lot, and I'm difficult to move.
12. I really don't see myself as being very important.
13. I don't often get too excited or enthusiastic about things.
14. I tend to repress my feelings.
15. I often give the appearance of being drained of energy.
16. I am often indecisive, not wanting to say 'yes' or 'no'.
17. I do all I can to preserve my energy.
18. I see myself as a mediator and a peacemaker.
19. I am not very punctual.
20. I like to have time to myself to just sit and do nothing.
21. My attention wanders a bit, so listening is difficult for me.
22. Never stand when you can sit, or sit when you can lie down!
23. In general I resign myself to the way things are.
24. I tend to be forgetful.
25. When you come right down to it, people don't differ all that much.

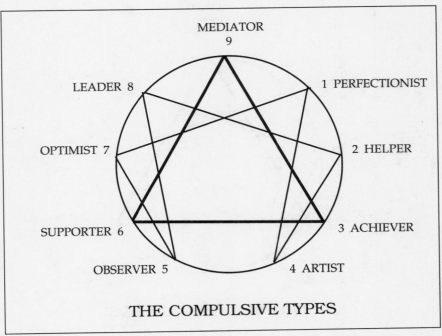

THE COMPULSIVE TYPES

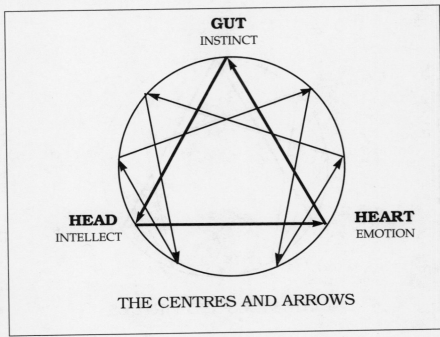

THE CENTRES AND ARROWS

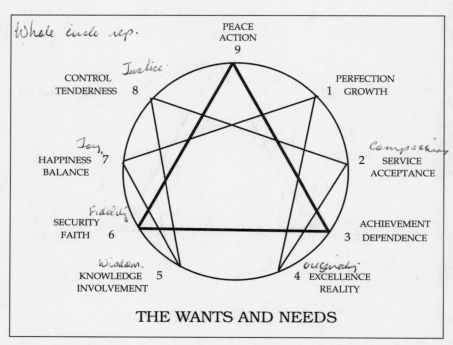

THE WANTS AND NEEDS

Labels around the diagram:

- PEACE / ACTION — 9
- CONTROL / TENDERNESS — 8 (*Justice*)
- PERFECTION / GROWTH — 1
- HAPPINESS / BALANCE — 7 (*Joy*)
- SERVICE / ACCEPTANCE — 2 (*Compassion*)
- SECURITY / FAITH — 6 (*Fidelity*)
- ACHIEVEMENT / DEPENDENCE — 3
- KNOWLEDGE / INVOLVEMENT — 5 (*Wisdom*)
- EXCELLENCE / REALITY — 4 (*originality*)

Whole circle rep.

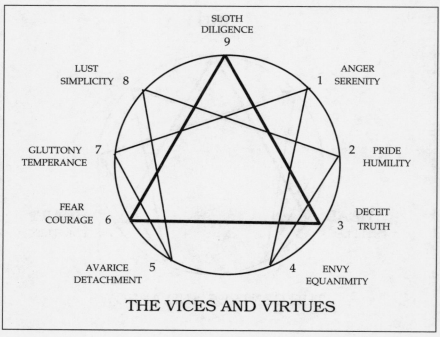

THE VICES AND VIRTUES

Labels around the diagram:

- SLOTH / DILIGENCE — 9
- LUST / SIMPLICITY — 8
- ANGER / SERENITY — 1
- GLUTTONY / TEMPERANCE — 7
- PRIDE / HUMILITY — 2
- FEAR / COURAGE — 6
- DECEIT / TRUTH — 3
- AVARICE / DETACHMENT — 5
- ENVY / EQUANIMITY — 4

16

ONES

Childhood:

ONES have lived all their lives with the expectations of others. The central message they receive as children is to work hard, be perfect and not be a 'bad' little child. They quickly learn what the rules are and try hard to put them into practice. By doing so they think their parents and other significant adults will love them. At the very least they will be complimented and given approval. With these rules they have a standard by which to judge others and know where they stand in any relationships they make. Criticism from parents can lead them to develop a negative self-image, become resentful and humourless, finding fault with everything.

Compulsion:

ONES can be good conversationalists and charming companions. But their obsession with perfection can make others feel uncomfortable in their presence. They are very orderly and meticulous. They are always on time. They work hard and methodically, and are frequently workaholics.

They avoid anger, deny its existence in them and, as far as

possible, keep their hostility in check. But it generally comes out as resentment, and is evident in the edginess of their speech and behaviour.

They feel they have to be right and to put others straight. In doing so, they are often intolerant, self-righteous and frequently make mountains out of molehills. Nothing is ever good enough - not even themselves. They are compelled to clean up the mess and impose order on what they see as chaos. They are sticklers for detail, checking and double-checking to make sure everything is correct, and frequently getting so bogged down in minutiae that they fail to see the wood for the trees.

They have a strong inner critical voice. They are generally rather up-tight and serious, continually trying to keep their emotions in control. There is never enough time in the day for them, and they become frustrated and even depressed when pressurized too much. They are very impatient and carry a 'hit list' of frustrations. They tend to be stubborn in getting their own way. They are often very tense and it is difficult for them to relax. They are compulsive about trying to meet all the demands others make on them, because only then do they feel they are loved.

Careers which suit their concern for rules and perfection include the law, the army, teaching, accountancy and medicine.

Conversion:

To achieve integration ONES need to take on the best aspects of the SEVEN. This will help them to:

■ *Relax and take things easy.* They are prone to take themselves too seriously and to overwork. They need to 'lighten up', take part in fun and games, and accept that this is good.

■ *Experience their anger.* They need to own their anger, while recognizing that they do not have to act out of it.

■ *Get in touch with their feelings*, especially the ones they are least happy with - the messy, chaotic and inappropriate ones which they seek to control. People are not condemned for having limitations. Indeed, true love means being accepted, faults and all.

■ *Stop judging themselves and others* by their hidden book of rules. They need to be less rigid and more patient.

■ *Appreciate the principle of growth.* Mistakes are a normal part of the way people grow to maturity. This is a process which takes time and cannot be rushed.

TWOS

NAME:	Helper
IDENTITY:	I'm caring
CENTRE:	Heart
COMPULSION:	Service
PASSION:	Pride
OUTLET:	Flattery
FEAR:	Being useless
REJECTION:	Own needs
DEFENCE:	Repression
FOCUS:	Empathy and Adapting
STANCE:	Bigger / Dependent
NEED:	To accept real worth
HEALING:	Gift / Grace
VIRTUE:	Humility

Childhood:

TWOS are always ready to help their parents with little tasks about the house. They are thoughtful and conscientious, see what needs to be done and do it. They light up when praised for this, and are ready to do more. They are sensitive to others feelings, and are prepared to sacrifice their own to please others. Consequently they are always welcome and well liked. This has always been the central demand made on them - to please others, to put others before self, not to contradict or disagree with whoever is in charge. As children TWOS quickly sense what others need, adapt themselves to meet these needs, and so gain approval and notice.

Compulsion:

TWOS are warm, sensitive and helpful people. They are capable of empathizing very well with the feelings of others, and of expressing emotion easily. The problem for them is that these feelings generally relate to others, rarely to themselves. They repress their own emotions and, while giving generously to others, deny that they have needs themselves. They get their identity from helping others, so that sometimes their service is less a concern for others than a way of being personally alive. They often have a 'me first' attitude.

They look for attention by responding to the real or imagined needs of others. To get this they can be manipulative. They rarely ask for favours directly. They expect others to notice what they need without having to be asked. If the other still does not notice and they badly need something they will flatter and manipulate to get what they want. When they are rejected in any way they adopt the martyr complex and become victims.

Since their greatest need is to be loved, they are also prone to infatuation. They are warm, caring people who love to touch and reach out to others. But they are so busy meeting the needs of others that they become out of touch with their own. Although their attention and warmth promise friendship, they find closeness and intimacy difficult. Their seductiveness and charm are meant not for real intimacy but for admiration and approval. Very compulsive TWOS can become hysterics - prone to over-dramatization, exhibitionism and exaggerated language.

Careers that attract TWOS are teaching, nursing, ministry, social service.

Conversion:

To achieve integration TWOS need to take on the best aspects of the FOUR . This will help them to:

■ *Get in touch with their own feelings and needs*, so that they can accept themselves as they really are. They are bad at recognizing their own needs and must own this and change it.

■ *Learn that love cannot be bought or earned*. Therefore they must curb their tendency to call attention to themselves by reminding others of the good they have done for them. This is always seen for what it is - an attempt to 'buy' affection.

■ *Know that they are lovable for who they are*. Unwillingness to change is grounded for them in their fear of not being loved. Their identity is so bound up with what others think of them that any change will take time.

■ *Appreciate their real worth* and understand that they do not have to gain approval by being either helpful or helpless. Their goal is partnership, not manipulation.

■ *Help others without ulterior motives*. They must not expect favours or expressions of gratitude for what they have done.

THREES

IDENTITY CARD

NAME:	Achiever
IDENTITY:	I'm successful
CENTRE:	Heart
COMPULSION:	Efficiency
PASSION:	Deceit
OUTLET:	Vanity
FEAR:	Failure
REJECTION:	Lying
DEFENCE:	Identification
FOCUS:	Image and Performance
STANCE:	Adjust / Aggressive
NEED:	Examine the Image
HEALING:	Depend on God's Will
VIRTUE:	Truth

Childhood:

THREES are busy and competitive little bees as children. They need to be, because all too often what they do is just not good enough for the significant adults in their lives. Performance is everything, they are told, so they try to make their parents proud of them by doing whatever it takes. Success and achievement are vital to them, because otherwise they feel they can neither be loved nor accepted. So they quickly find the things they are good at and which will get them attention. These they pursue, often to the neglect of their feelings and emotions. If not careful they can lose their sense of personal identity through over-identification with their role.

Compulsion:

The enthusiasm of the THREES makes them very attractive and the fact that they get things done means they are very much in demand. They are full of energy, creative, competitive and very productive. They are frequently referred to as being 'bright-eyed and bushy-tailed'. But their need to be successful and to be seen as such can lead them to neglect their feelings, become exploitative and opportunistic, and to bend the truth to their own ends. They are 'image makers' who prefer to dwell on the successful elements of their projects rather than on their drawbacks or even failures.

THREES are frequently workaholics. They revel in activity and can become hard taskmasters, being particularly dismissive of inefficiency, time-wasting and incompetence. They like to be in charge of projects but do not acknowledge other people's contributions to their success. If a project is likely to sink they make certain that they don't sink with it.

They wear a mask without knowing it is there. This extends to their feelings which they have learned to turn on to order. They feel what they are supposed to feel at the appropriate times. They are not comfortable revealing their feelings and avoid it by diverting attention to some interesting activity. Real intimacy is a problem for them and to avoid difficulties they give it a low priority. Action takes precedence over emotion for them, so they often seem distant and superficial.

THREES are good conversationalists, regularly telling people what will please or impress them. Since their image is all important, they dress well and for success. They have a very busy social life. They court popularity and love being in the public eye. A corollary to this is that they have no real sense of privacy - for themselves or others.

Given their talents they make excellent managers, administrators, and media/advertising executives.

Conversion:
To achieve integration THREES need to take on the best aspects of the SIX. This will help them to:

■ *Confront their deceptions.* They are great self-deceivers and need to learn that appearances are not everything.

■ *Develop the virtues of truthfulness and honesty.* This involves no bragging about their achievements, or exaggerating their importance so as to impress others.

■ *Slow down and take stock of their lives,* especially their relationships, activities, emotions and values. They need to accept that they are loved for who they are rather than for what they accomplish.

■ *Own and accept failures.* Only an inflated ego needs continual success. Being human makes them more desirable.

■ *Cooperate rather than compete with others.* There is no need to hog the limelight, put others down or make them feel inferior. They need to take the feelings of others into account.

FOURS

Childhood:

The FOURS see themselves as tragic figures, very different from everybody else. As children they may have lost a parent, been abandoned or felt abandoned. The joy in their lives is therefore brief, because they expect to be let down, disappointed and hurt. This personal sadness makes them so special that they think nobody else can understand their pain or loneliness. They learned the hard way that they couldn't count on their parents or other significant adults to be there when needed, either to comfort or support them. So they adopt the policy of rejecting others before they are rejected. They try to avoid emotional involvement, making up for it with a rich, symbolic fantasy life.

Compulsion:

The FOURS see themselves as special and are very sensitive to beauty in all its manifestations. They can be quite artistic and rely on imagery and symbols to describe their feelings and experiences. Nothing is ordinary in their lives. They have no time for the mundane or commonplace. Since even their joys and sorrows are either dramatic or tragic, they don't believe anyone else can experience life at their kind of depth. In this sense they can be emotional snobs, sometimes even being contemptuous or disdainful of the feelings of others. They see their attraction to beauty and their artistic good taste as compensating for their lack of self-esteem. They have style and dress accordingly.

Their imagination is very active and they like ritual and drama. They are often theatrical in their responses, frequently rehearsing conversations in their head before having them. In this sense, even though they desire spontaneity, they never achieve it. They imagine that if they were simple, down-to-earth individuals people would no longer love them or relate to them. Their fear that others will not understand them, and so will leave them alone, means that they get melancholic and sad. Indeed, they often seem to need to be mournful in order to feel alive. They analyse things to death, continually dwell on the past, and are subject to moodiness and depression. They are always attracted to what is outside their grasp, and never satisfied when it is theirs. They envy the fact that other people seem to possess what they lack. Manners, etiquette and good taste are important to them. They may clam up at times and harbour their negative feelings, but, like an oyster, they can also produce a pearl from a piece of grit.

FOURS tend to be actors, writers, musicians, poets and artists.

Conversion:
To achieve integration FOURS need to take on the best aspects of the ONE. This will help them to:

■ *Live in the present with all its troubles.* If they are ever to become happy and content they cannot remain fixed in idealizations and flights of fantasy.

■ *Stop envying others and making comparisons.* It will help them if they can see both the positive and negative elements in the things that happen.

■ *Accept that the self is not identical with feelings.* In particular, the presence of negative feelings does not mean the absence of positive ones.

■ *Use their talents productively,* no matter how insignificant their efforts may seem. They must not wait until they are in the mood but become active in the world as it is.

■ *Avoid rehearsing everything in their imagination,* especially when it involves over-romantic or negative feelings.

FIVES

Childhood:

Children who are FIVES are generally as quiet as mice. They retreat into themselves and keep their own counsel. But they also keep a close eye on what is going on around them. Often they play at being invisible so as not to attract attention. They perceive parents as overly intrusive, sometimes to the point where they seem to know what is going on even in the child's mind. They are not encouraged to become emotionally close. The family may have moved house often. FIVES learn to cope by pursuing privacy and living in the world of the mind. They read a lot but don't share their thoughts with others unless they have to. They know what's happening but protect themselves from involvement by getting lost in the crowd.

Compulsion:

FIVES have a great gift for getting to the heart of the matter and seeing the overall picture. The problem is that they find it very difficult to commit themselves and get involved. They are observers rather than participants. It is difficult to get to know them because they only give so much of themselves. They

25

compartmentalize their lives. They are very private and do not like their physical or mental space invaded. This gives them a detached and somewhat impersonal air.

Emotions are secondary to the FIVES. They isolate their feelings in order to give them time to come to a decision. If they are asked about their feelings they often talk about what they think. They are uncomfortable and sometimes embarrassed at parties, not having much skill at small talk. They frequently forget names and give the impresion of being stingy with their time and money. But, when they are interested, they can be very good listeners and, since they are eager to know everything they can, they are unusually open, receptive and non-judgemental.

They pursue knowledge to fill their inner emptiness. They never tell you everything they know, in case it drains their resources. Moreover, they rarely think they have much that is worth saying - their knowledge is never sufficiently complete and comprehensive to warrant it. Hence they can find themselves taking endless courses in order to increase their store of knowledge and to avoid getting involved in the nuts and bolts of day-to-day activity. They are forever preparing themselves. Since they generally desire anonymity, preferring to blend in rather than stand out, they are not seen as a threat, yet they can be both profound and provocative.

Given their talents they make good hermits, researchers, interviewers, librarians and counsellors.

Conversion:
To achieve integration FIVES need to take on the best aspects of the EIGHT. This will help them to:

■ *Become involved and committed.* They need to become active and 'doers', not just observers or theoreticians.

■ *Share more of themselves.* To counterbalance their avarice and possessiveness they need to risk self-disclosure and share more in terms of time, knowledge and money.

■ *Recognize that emotions, too, give insight.* Self-knowledge is not limited to theories and analysis.

■ *Trust others and cooperate more.* This will help open them up emotionally and allow them to experience companionship.

■ *Avoid jumping to conclusions.* Theorizing at the drop of a hat can contribute to poor judgement. Though it may be difficult for them, they should consult someone whose judgement they respect.

SIXES

Childhood:

SIXES go through childhood with antennae on permanent alert. They have a highly developed sense of danger and grow up experiencing a great deal of fear. The ten commandments may have been drummed into them, with the emphasis on all the *Don'ts*. They may even have been threatened with the 'Boogie Man'. As a result, they quickly learn to be cautious, careful, wary and suspicious. Not having received much encouragement to succeed they develop a low self-esteem. They respond to the threat of danger in two basic ways. The first is to avoid it by becoming very obedient, conformist and conscientious. The second is to face and attempt to defuse it. This can sometimes lead to anger which expresses itself in delinquent behaviour. Their instinct for survival leads them to be very much in touch with their feelings and those of others.

Compulsion:

Because of their early experiences, SIXES are plagued by both fear and doubt about themselves and others. They are so cautious that they have great difficulty in making decisions.

They see all the possible snags and these inhibit their action. They much prefer to be told what to do by someone in a position of authority rather than risk making decisions themselves. They are, therefore, very good party people, loyal to whatever group they have joined, obeying the rules and keen to ensure that others do the same. They like the sense of solidarity and support which belonging to a group brings. Though sometimes they think the group demands too much of them, they also find it hard to tolerate it when others buck the system with apparent impunity. When they themselves deviate from the rules, they can't admit it and use denial and projection to cover their shame. They tend to spot the mote in someone else's eye while overlooking the beam in their own.

It is important for SIXES to know who belongs and who does not. Equally important is their precise rank and power within the group. They are generally mistrustful of anyone purporting to help them, and are quick to notice interlopers with hidden agendas. They do not like it when others question their opinions and sometimes resort to aggressive behaviour to counter what they see as essentially a threat. Basically they are insecure. They are frequently secretive and rather tense people, for whom life is very serious. Whenever they do a good job they find it difficult to accept the credit. However, having lived with fear all their lives, they readily identify with the underdogs and courageously champion their causes.

SIXES frequently choose the church, the law or the armed forces as careers.

Conversion:

To achieve integration SIXES need to take on the best aspects of the NINE. This will help them to:

■ *Become calmer and more peaceful*, rather than fearful and full of doubt. It is vital that they believe that there is nothing that can destroy their deepest selves

■ *Trust others more and become less suspicious*. When they let others know they love them, they are loved in return. There *is* enough love to go around.

■ *Take responsibility for their own actions*, instead of pretending to be obeying orders. They need to become more their own person and stop hiding behind the shield of authority.

■ *Avoid overreacting*. In times of stress and anxiety they need to control their fear about the imagined outcome.

■ *Be more direct in communicating*. This involves being open and clear about feelings, and not giving mixed signals.

SEVENS

IDENTITY CARD

NAME:	Optimist
IDENTITY:	I'm happy
CENTRE:	Head
COMPULSION:	Optimism
PASSION:	Gluttony
OUTLET:	Planning
FEAR:	Pain
REJECTION:	Pain
DEFENCE:	Rationalization
FOCUS:	Fun and Plans
STANCE:	Smaller / Dependent
NEED:	Balance
HEALING:	God's Creative Helpers
VIRTUE:	Temperance

Childhood:

As children SEVENS are cheerful, enthusiastic little extroverts - attractive, amusing, full of charm and fun, forever on the go. But this masks the fact that deep down they are frightened and afraid. In an attempt to diffuse their pain and divert their attention to other more pleasant things, they move out toward people. In later life they have very selective memories about their childhood, remembering only the good times, shutting out the bad. There may be many reasons for their feeling fearful - parents who don't ever want them to grow up; the loss of someone or something; parental unemployment or family poverty. Whatever it is, the child makes up for it with an overactive imagination and lifestyle which concentrates on the positive and superficial, allowing no time to come to terms with the negative and unpleasant realities of life.

Compulsion:

SEVENS are gregarious, cheerful, optimistic and full of energy. But they will do anything they can to avoid pain in all its forms. Living is meant to be enjoyable, so they make sure they are always on the go and have a full programme of activities lined up. This ensures that they keep out of the line of fire. They want to see, do and experience everything. Consequently they don't pursue things with the kind of single-mindedness often needed to rise to the top. Having a multitude of friends and activities means that the loss of one does not create an empty hole which cannot be filled. It has the added advantage that they will never be bored. They are excellent conversation-alists, with a fund of stories.

The variety of interests and speed with which they move about burns up their energies, giving them an excuse for not dealing with deeper and more complex personal, social and spiritual issues. This means that they find commitment to causes or to people difficult to maintain. SEVENS are free spirits who hate to be tied down or to make priority choices. They are superficial rather than deep and can be narcissistic. They dislike confrontation and generally run away from it by involving themselves in more pleasant activities or even in addictive behaviour.

They are frequently 'con artists' who can charm the birds from the trees. They always have Plan B up their sleeve, with enough loopholes in both it and Plan A to allow them to escape if need be. They tend to be dreamers and future-orientated but want instant gratification, and can become very aggressive indeed when others try to set limits to their self-indulgence, forcing them to exercise restraint and self-control.

Given their talents they make good entertainers, musicians and writers (science fiction and children's stories).

Conversion:

To achieve integration SEVENS need to take on the best aspects of the FIVE. This will help them to:

■ *Get to the heart of the matter*, rather than remain on the surface and risk being forever superficial.

■ *Give rather than take.* They need to temper their thirst for instant gratification and 'grab now' mentality and learn to contribute rather than consume.

■ *Face the pain, not seek to avoid it.* They must stop trivializing serious issues. Making fun of problems will not make them go away or contribute towards a solution.

■ *Control their impulsive nature.* It is important to know which enthusiasms to act on and which to control.

■ *Learn the value of solitude and silence.* Their constant need for distractions and stimulation needs checking.

EIGHTS

Childhood:

Children who are EIGHTS quickly intuit that they can become the boss by denying their fear and vulnerability and using their power. They learn that if they assert themselves aggressively enough they can dictate the rules of the game and always get their way. Shouting, anger, vandalism and other such tactics allow them to dominate parents and others without any really painful comeback. Since we all imagine that other people are no different from ourselves, EIGHTS think that others also enjoy standing up for themselves. Consequently, they pay little attention to the feelings of others, refuse to say they're sorry and never ask for forgiveness. They learn to deny their feelings of guilt, and are quick to exploit any weakness they see. Always spoiling for a fight, they sometimes end up as delinquents.

Compulsion:

EIGHTS are the most aggressive of all the types and love to confront, intimidate and dominate others. They see life as a struggle to become 'topdog' and in the process can ruthlessly put other people down, especially by attacking them at their weakest point. They say 'no' more readily than 'yes'. They can be scathing in their criticisms and coarse in their use of language. They are self-assertive attention-getters and bulldoze their way through others if given half a chance. They despise weakness and only respect those who are ready to stand up for themselves.

However, they are also willing to take risks and stand up for the 'underdog', particularly when they are the victims of injustice or oppression. At their best they see justice as an important value. If they are convinced that something is right they will be fiercely courageous in championing it. They work with zeal and intensity when they are involved in a project. They love a challenge and don't count the cost. They are very protective of their friends and of those in their care, but their relationships are generally based on possessiveness and submission.

Anger is their way of getting at the truth. They provoke people to find out what makes them tick. It is important to them that they be in control of people and events. They do not like surprises, especially in dealing with people. They like to get things out in the open and are highly confrontational. If they are dissatisfied with something, they will say so. They do not like pretence, deception or underhanded methods and constantly seek to expose and unmask these in others.

With their talents they may become public prosecutors, chief executives, missionaries, or even dictators.

Conversion:

To achieve integration EIGHTS need to take on the best aspects of the TWO. This will help them to:

■ *Acknowledge that others have rights too*. They must not be ignored, bullied, taken advantage of or dominated.

■ *Own the tender side of their nature*. Growth happens when they accept their gentler feelings and reveal their wounds and weaknesses. This is a sign of real strength.

■ *Accept that no one can be self-sufficient*. Dependence on others is part of being human, and acknowledging that means letting others take control and appreciating their help.

■ *Learn to use their power for people* rather than against them. This involves standing up for others, fighting their battles and inspiring them to stand on their own two feet.

■ *Develop their magnanimity and generosity*. Self-interest is not the goal of life and money is more than a power tool.

NINES

IDENTITY CARD

NAME:	Mediator
IDENTITY:	I'm easy-going
CENTRE:	Gut
COMPULSION:	Inaction
PASSION:	Laziness
OUTLET:	Indolence
FEAR:	Conflict
REJECTION:	Conflict
DEFENCE:	Narcotization
FOCUS:	Peace and Conflict
STANCE:	Adjust / Withdrawing
NEED:	Action
HEALING:	Love
VIRTUE:	Diligence

Childhood:

Typically, nothing really matters to NINES, least of all themselves. This is because they seem to be continually overlooked by parents or other significant adults. They are not really listened to and cannot even get attention by becoming angry. Brothers or sisters may be preferred to them.They interpret all this as saying that they are not important enough to be loved and they cope with it by denying their own worth. Even at this early stage NINES compensate for an apparent lack of affection by turning to substitutes - excessive eating, reading and watching television. They are often placid, easy-going children, whose colourless appearance and voice indicate that they don't have much self-esteem. They learn not to bother, not to make an effort and not to show their anger.

Compulsion:

NINES are very easy-going and prone to indecision and indolence. Yet they expend a great deal of energy trying to avoid conflict. They are the great 'peacemakers'. They want harmony, and are willing to resign themselves to difficult situations

33

and play down problems rather than face the aggravation of dealing with them. They regularly buy time to get out of making decisions, and are even ready to make "molehills out of mountains" in order to maintain the peace.

Since nothing matters all that much and nobody is more important than anyone else, NINES are generally unshockable. They are very tolerant and accepting of people, no matter how awkward or difficult. They are non-judgemental and non-threatening, always willing to balance one view with another. They are unassuming and receptive and are, therefore, very comfortable and calming to be with. However, although they like you, they give the impression that they would like someone else just as well. They daydream a lot.

They are sometimes surprisingly busy people, but they concern themselves with doing non-essential things since they find it hard to distinguish between these and what is really important. They find it difficult to decide on priorities or to keep focussed. Since they try not to get excited about things, time just passes them by. Being late doesn't bother them and they are often forgetful. They procrastinate a lot. They love being rooted in their own space.

They don't trust themselves. Though they have undoubted talents, they are uneasy with compliments. They prefer to remain out of the limelight in case people begin to expect too much from them. They need to remain in control and for that reason don't like surprises. They can 'dig in' and become quite stubborn, but generally keep their anger in check.

The NINES make excellent negotiators, mediators, counsellors and facilitators.

Conversion:

To achieve integration NINES need to take on the best aspects of the THREE. This will help them to:

■ *Acknowledge their own self-worth.* This is their greatest need. They cannot love and appreciate others if they do not love and appreciate themselves.

■ *Take control of their lives.* They need to rouse themselves out of their complacency and become involved in life.

■ *Face the tensions and conflicts,* and avoid trying to make things peaceful and tranquil at any price.

■ *Deal with negative feelings,* and not try to paper over the cracks. They need to own their aggression and stubbornness.

■ *Confront all forms of narcotization and escapism.* Life is full of problems and tranquillizers are no solution.